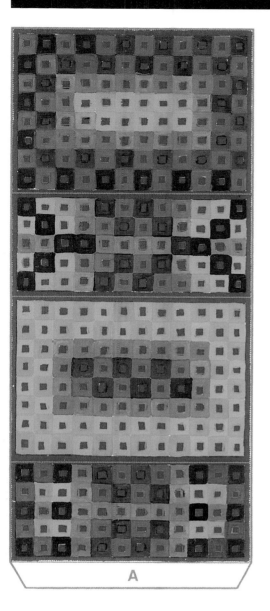

A

B

D   E

A

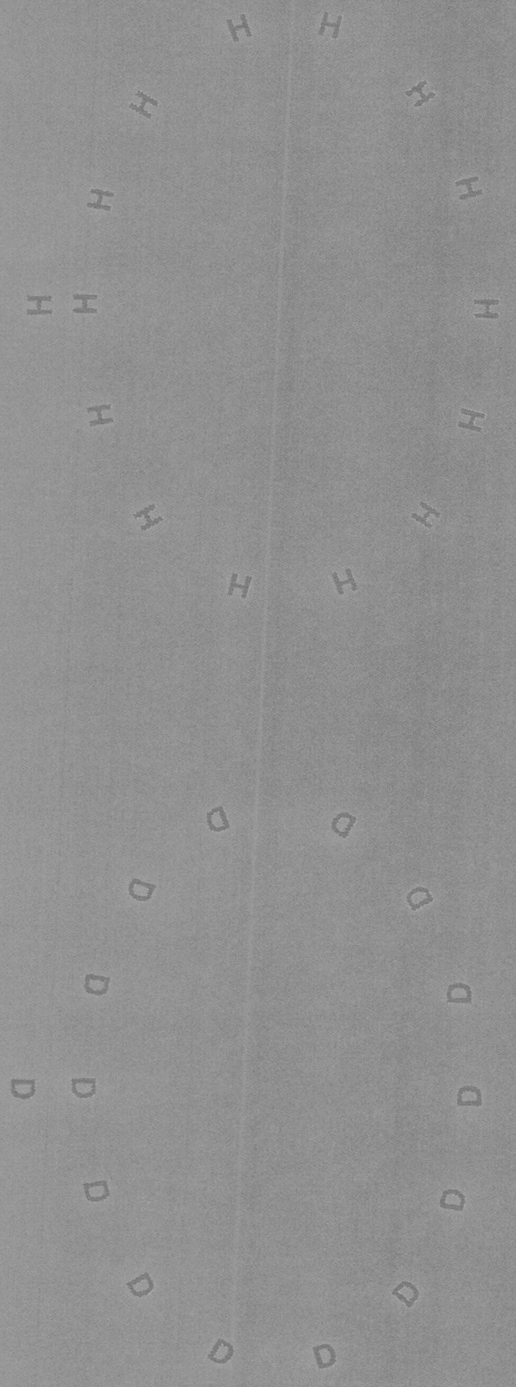

H
H
H
H
H
H
H
H
H
H
H
H
H
H
H
H
H

D
D
D
D
D
D
D
D
D
D
D
D

E   A

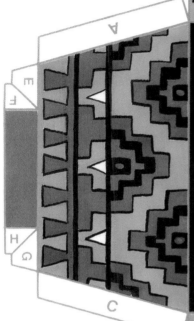

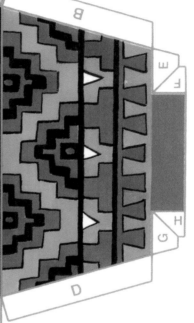

The other piece of the Herbal box
is on the next page.

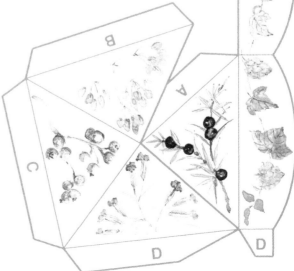

The other piece of the Herbal box is on the previous page.

All gift boxes, whatever their shape, start as a plan or net marked out on a card of suitable thickness. To design your own gift boxes you have first to draw the net itself. Some people like to draw their nets once only on the card they are going to use, others prefer to work first on paper and then to transfer it to the card by tracing or by using carbon paper.

HOW TO DESIGN GIFT BOXES OF YOUR OWN

Let us begin by thinking about the net of a simple box like the one given here. We can use it to point out some of the basic techniques which are needed to get good results

1. Use a sharp pencil, ruler and set square to set out a basic network of fine lines on which the net will be drawn. Draw all the lines longer than you need. The surplus can be rubbed out or cut off when the net is complete.

2. Mark out equal distances with compasses and not by measuring with a ruler. This will always give better results.

3. Flaps are very important, both as a means to glue the box together, but also to make the lid fit well. The flaps should not be less than 7mm wide and perhaps a little larger for bigger boxes.

(a) Flaps which are to be glued should be cut to 60°

(b) Flaps which will be seen when the box is used for gifts should be rounded off with compasses.

4. A thumb hole gives the box a professional finish and makes it easier to open.

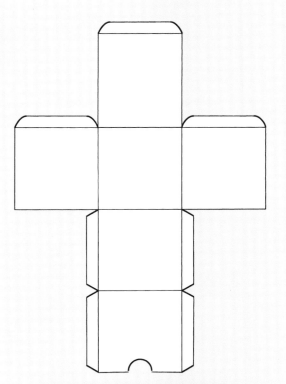

THE NET OF A CUBE - SHAPED BOX WITH AN ATTACHED LID

SPECIAL ADVICE

THE CARD TO USE
The boxes in "More Gift Boxes!" were printed on 250gsm card. The unit "gsm" means "grammes per square metre" and is the way that the weight or thickness of card or paper is measured. If you intend to buy new card to make some boxes of your own, then you need card of 200gsm or heavier. The larger you want the boxes to be, the thicker the card you need. Since most people will probably be using card which they already have, then it is a simple matter to do some trials.

THE IMPORTANCE OF SCORING
To get good results, the edges of the boxes need to be sharp and straight and that means scoring. The simplest method of scoring is to rule along the fold lines with a ball-point pen which has run out of ink. Experienced model makers can use a craft knife, but it needs care not to cut right through the card. After scoring, crease firmly along all the fold lines.

DECORATION
Perhaps the card which you have is attractive in itself and then the boxes can be made with a minimum of additional decoration. However it is always nice to add personal touches. If the card is plain, then you can add designs to the faces using felt-tip pens, paints or pastels. Whether you prefer to decorate before glueing together or afterwards depends really on how complicated you want the design to be. Don't forget the possibility of glueing cut-out patterns or pressed flowers to the lids or sides of the boxes. You can get some lovely effects that way.

LIDS AND FASTENINGS
A fascinating part of designing gift boxes is to work out interesting lids and interesting ways of fastening them. A space of about 1mm all round seems to be about the right amount for a neatly fitting lid, but thicker cards may need a little more. Apart from the ideas you have already met in "More Gift Boxes! ", there are sure to be many different boxes and packets in any kitchen or storeroom. You might well be able to get some good ideas for your own designs by seeing how commercial boxes are made.

GIFT BOXES WITH SLIDING DRAWERS

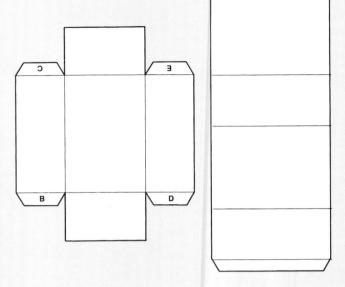

A type of box which uses a method of construction which is very similar to a simple cube is a rectangular box with a sliding drawer. Make the dimensions of the drawer about 1mm less in each direction so that it slides easily but not too loosely.

It is usual to push a matchbox to open it and this is the natural way to open gift boxes of this type. However you might like to try an alternative and to make a fancy handle on the drawer either out of paper or some fine string or coloured wool.

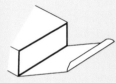

People who like to make more complicated boxes could add side flaps to the wrapper which tuck in. Then they have to be opened before the drawer will slide out. A double surprise!

If you can make a little scene inside the sliding drawer then your gift box can become a gift itself. In the past people sometimes used to make wonderful minature scenes in boxes like this as very special presents. Some almost became tiny doll's houses. There is no need to make the scene as complicated as that, but do your best to think of something which is suitable for the person you are giving it to.

OPEN TOPPED BOXES - CARD VASES

The Greek Pot is a good example of a box with no lid, yet which does not give the impression that it is unfinished.

Notice how to constuct the net of a box which has sloping sides. You can experiment with different radii and angles and see how the shape of the finished box changes. The Greek Pot has six sides so the opening is a hexagon. You might like to contruct a box with five sides giving a pentagonal opening or a box with eight sides which gives an opening which is an octagon.

If you want to make a more unusual shape, make one with seven sides.

To get the angle at the centre, in order to draw a regular polygon, divide the number of sides into 360°.

5	6	7	8
72°	60°	51.3°	45°

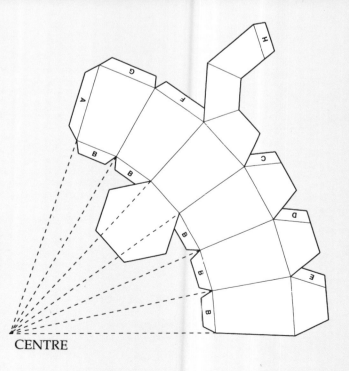

CENTRE

If you can find some coloured tissue paper, then wrap the present in it and push it inside the open topped box in a casual or informal way.

CIRCULAR AND OVAL GIFT BOXES

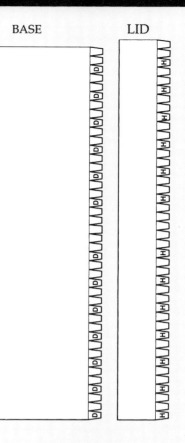

BASE   LID

LID

BASE

The Arabesque box is a very attactive one and it is based on a true ellipse or oval. Ovals are quite hard to draw unless you use a template or stencil, but it is possible to make very charming circular boxes by using compasses. Make the radius of the lid about 1mm greater than the base.

Circular lids and bases have to be glued to the sides by means of snip-strips and it is best to add them to the rectangular sides as shown on the diagrams. Not only is it easier to draw them evenly, but the lid will not snag as you put it on.

Draw the length of each rectangular side to be seven times the radius of the circle and this will give a suitable overlap. You will need to trim off the last few snip-strips so that there is not a double layer.

GIFT BOXES WITH "POP-ENDS"

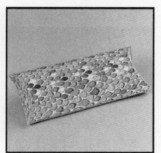

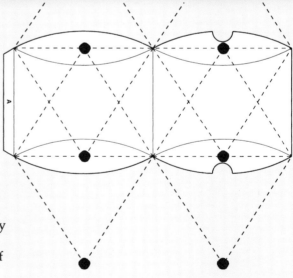

● CENTRES OF THE ARCS

Each of the pop-ends of this type of box is made of two equal arcs drawn with compasses. The diagram on the right shows how to constuct them. It is best to experiment with different radii because if the ends are too deep the the box looks clumsy and if they are too shallow then it will only hold a very small present . All the four centres lie on the central line of each half and of course keep the same radius for all eight arcs.

If you have some attractive wrapping paper which would look good for this kind of box, but which is too thin to use on its own then glue to some suitable card first. Draw the net on the inside and then there will be no lines showing on the outside. If you are going to paint or decorate plain card yourself it is best for the net to be on the outside also. Do the construction lines as faintly as you can.

Note how the finger holes on the inner leaf makes the box very much easier to open.

Pop-end boxes can be made from a single net or as two pieces which are identical except for the finger holes.

GIFT BOXES WHICH ARE ANTIPRISMS

Two of the boxes in this book belong to the very special kind of shape called an antiprism. Notice that the lid and the base are both the same shape but that their edges are not parallel but are rotated relative to each other by the triangular sides. A prism is a shape where the ends are the same shape but their edges remain parallel.

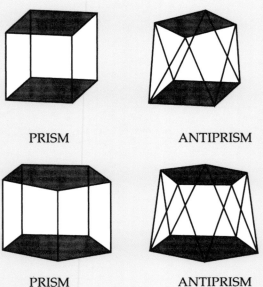

PRISM ANTIPRISM

PRISM ANTIPRISM

ANTIPRISMS WITH SLOPING SIDES

Since gift boxes which are antiprisms are such attrative shapes you might like to experiment with similar boxes where the lid is smaller than the base.

The net on the right shows such a box where the lid is 70% of the size of the base. The triangular sides must now be uneven because it is not possible for all of them to be isosceles, but the lid must still fit. Experiment and see what you can discover.

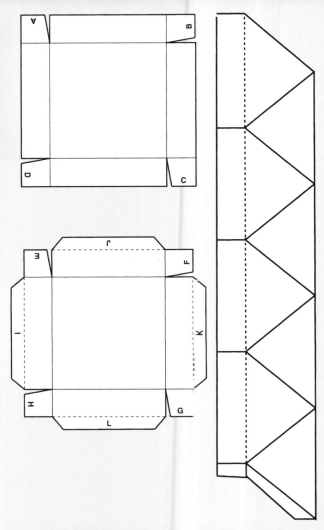

You might care to design an antiprism box with its lid and base each a regular pentagon. It will have 10 triangles and the lid will be rotated by 36° relative to the base. The 36° is half the 72° which is the angle at the centre of a pentagon.

If you like this kind of shape try to make a gift box which is a hexagonal antiprism. How many triangles will it have and what is the angle of rotation?

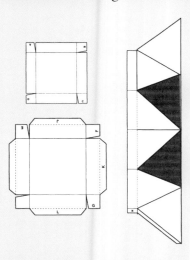

If you have enjoyed making these boxes then there may be other Tarquin books which would interest you, including 'The Gift Box Book' also by Gerald Jenkins and Anne Wild. Tarquin books are available from Bookshops, Toyshops, Art/Craft Shops and in case of difficulty directly by post from the publishers.
For an up-to-date catalogue please write to Tarquin Publications, Stradbroke, Diss, Norfolk, IP21 5JP, England.

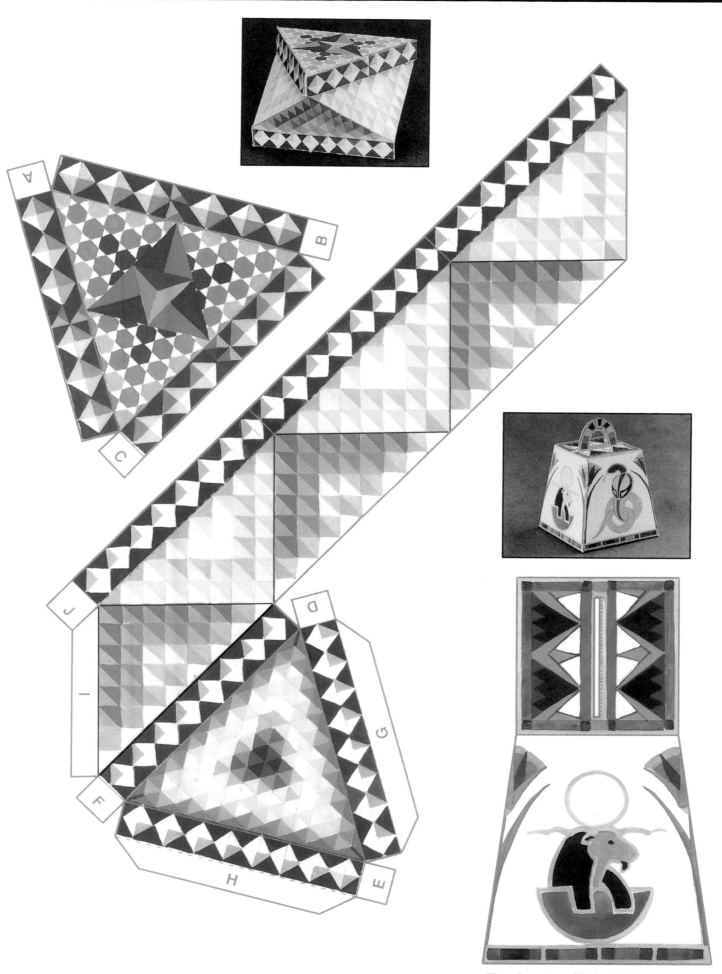

The other piece of Ptolmey's box
is on the next page.

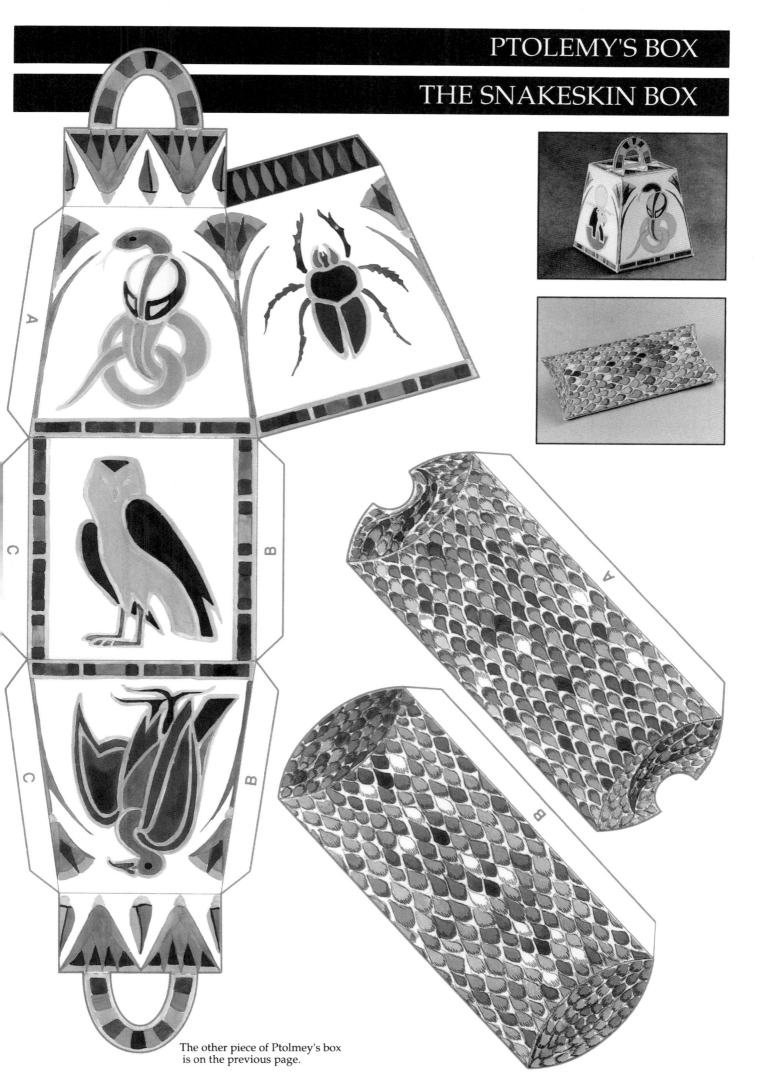

The other piece of Ptolmey's box
is on the previous page.

B

B

B

A

THE STENCILLED BOX

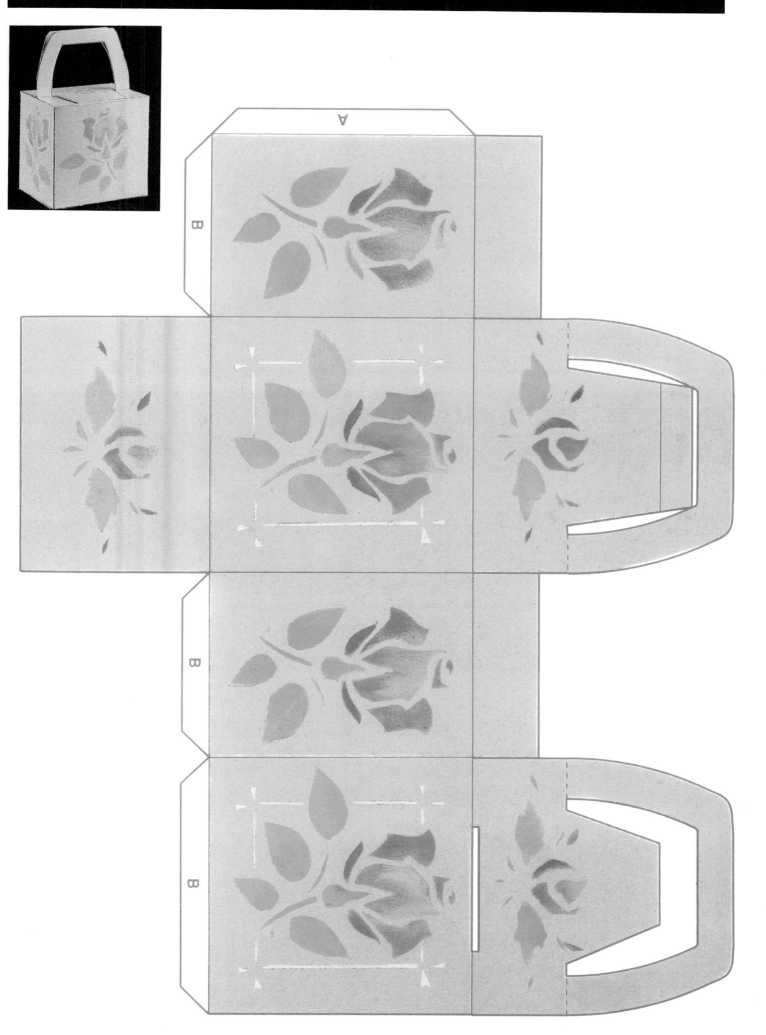

A

B

B

B

A